Is it the same or different?

Bobbie Kalman

Crabtree Publishing Company

www.crabtreebooks.com

Created by Bobbie Kalman

Dedicated by Andrea Crabtree
For my beautiful friend Lydia, with love

**Author and
Editor-in-Chief**
Bobbie Kalman

Editors
Reagan Miller
Robin Johnson

Photo research
Crystal Sikkens

Design
Bobbie Kalman
Katherine Kantor
Samantha Crabtree (cover)

Production coordinator
Katherine Kantor

Illustrations
Barbara Bedell: pages 14, 15, 24 (giraffe and porcupine)
Katherine Kantor: page 24 (snake)

Photographs
© Dreamstime.com: pages 19 (bottom), 23 (bottom), 24 (fish)
© iStockphoto.com: front cover, pages 19 (top), 20 (middle)
© ShutterStock.com: pages 1, 3, 4, 5, 6, 7, 8, 9, 10, 11, 12, 13 (except
        butterfly), 14, 15, 16, 17, 18, 20 (top), 21 (fly and cat eyes), 22,
        23 (top and middle), 24 (all except dog and fish)
Other images by Creatas, Digital Vision, and Photodisc

Library and Archives Canada Cataloguing in Publication

Kalman, Bobbie, 1947-
    Is it the same or different? / Bobbie Kalman.

(Looking at nature)
Includes index.
ISBN 978-0-7787-3317-1 (bound).--ISBN 978-0-7787-3337-9 (pbk.)

    1. Visual perception--Juvenile literature. 2. Nature--Juvenile
literature. I. Title. II. Series: Looking at nature (St. Catharines, Ont.)

QA174.5.K34 2007   j508   C2007-904245-7

Library of Congress Cataloging-in-Publication Data

Kalman, Bobbie.
    Is it the same or different? / Bobbie Kalman.
        p. cm. -- (Looking at nature)
    ISBN-13: 978-0-7787-3317-1 (rlb)
    ISBN-10: 0-7787-3317-3 (rlb)
    ISBN-13: 978-0-7787-3337-9 (pb)
    ISBN-10: 0-7787-3337-8 (pb)
    Includes an index.
    1. Animals--Miscellanea--Juvenile literature. 2. Animals--Classification-
-Juvenile literature. I. Title. II. Series.

QL49.K2945 2008
590.1'2--dc22

2007027220

Crabtree Publishing Company

www.crabtreebooks.com   1-800-387-7650

**Published in Canada
Crabtree Publishing**
616 Welland Ave.
St. Catharines, Ontario
L2M 5V6

**Published in the United States
Crabtree Publishing**
PMB16A
350 Fifth Ave., Suite 3308
New York, NY 10118

**Published in the United Kingdom
Crabtree Publishing**
White Cross Mills
High Town, Lancaster
LA1 4XS

**Published in Australia
Crabtree Publishing**
386 Mt. Alexander Rd.
Ascot Vale (Melbourne)
VIC 3032

Contents

Look closely!   4

Same or different?   6

Are they birds?   8

Be it a bee?   10

Are these snakes?   12

Long necks?   14

A cup of what?   16

Ouch! That is sharp!   18

Are eyes the same?   20

A lot of leopards!   22

Words to know and Index   24

Look closely!

Things in our world may look the same. Things in our world may look different. Look closely at the things around you. Some things may be the same in some ways, but they may be very different in other ways. Look at the animals on this page. They are all cats. How are they the same? How are they different?

lynx cub

pet kitten

tiger cub

4

The animals on this page are all **insects**. Insects are small animals with six legs. Some insects have wings. Look at all these insects. There are two of each kind of insect. Which insects are the same?

(1) butterfly

(2) dragonfly

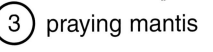

(3) praying mantis

(4)

(6)

Answers:
1 is the same as 4
2 is the same as 5
3 is the same as 6

(5)

Same or different?

This animal has white fur on its back. It also has some brown fur on its body. What can this animal be? Will it show itself to me?

Is this the same animal, or is it a different one?
Look at both pictures. Give reasons why you think
this lemur is the same animal as the one on page 6.

Are they birds?

A hummingbird is a small bird. It drinks **nectar**. Nectar is a sweet liquid in flowers. A hummingbird's long beak can reach the nectar in flowers. To stay in place while it drinks, a hummingbird flaps its wings quickly.

The animal below is also drinking nectar from a flower. It flaps its wings very fast, too. Is this animal a hummingbird? No, this animal is not a bird. It is an insect called a hummingbird moth. How do you think this insect got its name?

bird

moth

Be it a bee?

Bees are black insects with yellow stripes on their bodies. Bees have wings for flying. They visit flowers for nectar. Bees drink nectar and also use it to make honey. This bee is visiting a yellow flower.

This animal has yellow stripes, too. It is looking at some yellow flowers. Is it the same as a bee, or is it different? Can this animal fly? Can it make honey? No, it cannot make honey. This animal is a dog, not a bee!

Are these snakes?

This green snake is hiding among some leaves. It has a long body and smooth skin. Does it see another green snake on the next page? Do you see one?

Is this animal a green snake? Can a snake turn into a butterfly? No, it cannot, but a caterpillar can! This animal is a caterpillar, not a snake.

Long necks?

A giraffe has a very long neck and four long legs. It is a tall animal! A giraffe's brown fur has white markings on it. Giraffes live in hot, grassy places.

This animal's long body looks like a giraffe's neck. Its skin is also brown with white markings. Is this animal a giraffe? No, this animal is a moray eel. A moray eel is a fish that lives in the ocean. It has no neck. It has no legs. A moray eel has a long, thin body like the body of a snake.

moray eel

a giraffe's coat

A cup of what?

All these animals are small. They are so small that they can fit into teacups! How are these animals the same? How are they different?

This little animal is a dog. A dog has four legs. It has fur on its body.

This animal is a duck. A duck is a bird. Birds have two legs and two wings. Birds have feathers.

This cup has a frog in it.
A frog has four legs.
A frog has slimy skin.
A frog does not have fur
or feathers on its body.

This furry little hamster
has four legs. Which other
animal has fur and four
legs? Which animal is
most like this hamster?

Ouch! That is sharp!

Porcupines are animals that have **quills** on their bodies. Quills are sharp needles. The quills keep porcupines safe from other animals. If an animal attacks a porcupine, the porcupine's quills get stuck in the animal's body. Ouch!

This animal has sharp
needles on its body, too.
When the animal is afraid,
it fills its body with water,
and its needles stick
out. Is this animal the
same as the porcupine
on page 18? No, this
animal is a porcupine fish.

Are eyes the same?

Look at the eyes on these pages. Are they the same or different? One pair of eyes is not real. Which eyes are not real eyes?

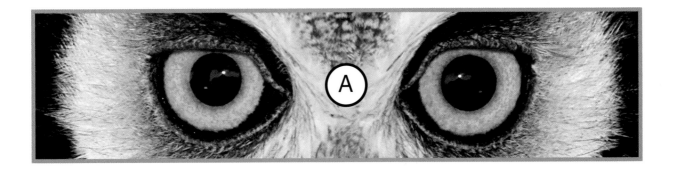

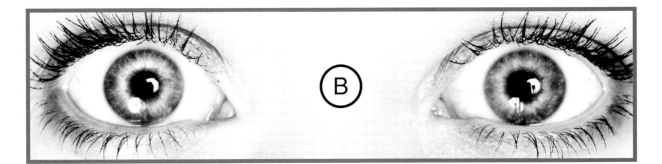

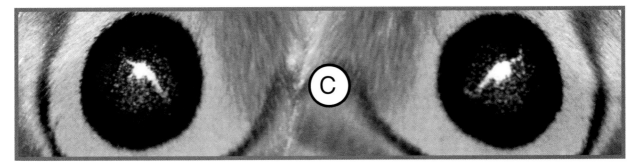

Each pair of eyes belongs to
an animal listed below. Match
the eyes to the correct animal.

1. moth   4. frog
2. fly   5. owl
3. child   6. cat

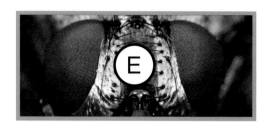

The spots on the moth's wings are not
eyes. The spots are called **eyespots**.
They look like eyes, but the moth
does not use these eyes to see.

Answers:

6. cat–F
5. owl–A
4. frog–D
3. child–B
2. fly–E
1. moth–C

21

A lot of leopards!

Leopards are wild cats. Leopards have many spots on their fur. This leopard cub is covered in spots. Some other animals have the word "leopard" in their names. Are they the same as this leopard cub, or are they different?